COLUMBUS' FIRST VOYAGE

LATIN SELECTIONS FROM
PETER MARTYR'S *DE ORBE NOVO*

Edited for Studen

Constance P. Iacona & Edward V. George

Bolchazy-Carducci Publishers, Inc.
Mundelein, Illinois USA

Co-Editors
LeaAnn A. Osburn
Vicki Wine

Typography, Page and Cover Design
Adam Phillip Velez

Cover Illustration
Spanish Vessel

Columbus' First Voyage
Latin Selections from Peter Martyr's *De Orbe Novo*

by Constance P. Iacona and Edward V. George

Bolchazy-Carducci Publishers, Inc.
1570 Baskin Road
Mundelein, IL 60060 USA
www.bolchazy.com

Printed in the United States of America
2010
by CreateSpace

ISBN 978-0-86516-613-4

Library of Congress Cataloging-in-Publication Data

Anghiera, Pietro Martire d', 1457-1526.
  [De orbe novo. Selections]
  Columbus' first voyage : Latin selections from Peter Martyr's De Orbe Novo /
edited for students by Constance P. Iacona and Edward V. George.
     p. cm.
  Text in Latin with critical apparatus and additional text in English.
  ISBN-13: 978-0-86516-613-4 (pbk. : alk. paper)
  ISBN-10: 0-86516-613-7 (pbk. : alk. paper)
  1. Latin language, Medieval and modern--Readers. 2. Columbus,
Christopher--Early works to 1800. 3. America--Early accounts to
1600.   I. Iacona, Constance P. II. George, E. (Edward), 1937-   .
III. Title. IV. Title: Columbus' 1st voyage.
PA2905.A54 2005
478.6'421--dc22

                                                              2005023701

CONTENTS

ILLUSTRATIONS

Figures 1, 3, 5, 6, and 7 are reprinted from *The Letter of Columbus on the Discovery of America. A Facsimile of The Pictoral Edition, with a New and Literal Translation and a Complete Reprint of The Oldest Four Editions in Latin.* (New York: Trustees of the Lenox Library, 1892)

PREFACE

Latin programs usually start by assuming that practically all Latin writings which deserve attention come from classical antiquity, more specifically from the two centuries before and after the birth of Christ. We do not dispute the central place of the ancient classics. But we contend that this narrow focus on the ancient world leaves out a vast reservoir of valuable writings. Broad areas of achievement, extending through the Middle Ages, the Renaissance, and the modern world, are overlooked. It is time to widen the scope of what we introduce in Latin classes.[1]

The following excerpts from Peter Martyr's *De Orbe Novo*, or *On the New World*, narrating Columbus' first voyage to America, form just one sample from the rich vein of source material in Latin for illustrating Hispanic America.[2] Peter Martyr of Angleria's terse, lucid reports of the early Spanish adventures in the western hemisphere combine readability, significant content, and particular interest for an American audience. His chronicles remain some of the most important sources for the history of early Spanish exploration and colonization.

Citations from Cristoforo Colombo, *Epistola de Insulis Nuper Inventis: Latin Text and Translation* by Frank E. Robbins (Ann Arbor: University Microfilms, Inc., 1966) abbreviated in the Background Notes as "Columbus Letter" are reprinted with permission of ProQuest Information and Learning Company. Further reproduction is prohibited without permission. We are also grateful for permission to quote from *The Diario of Christopher Columbus's First Voyage to America, 1492–1493*. Translated and edited by Oliver C. Dunn and James E. Kelley, Jr. Published by the University of Oklahoma Press, 1989. Reprinted by permission of the publisher.

---

1 See the elaboration of our viewpoint in Terence Tunberg, "Latinitas: The Misdiagnosis of Latin's Rigor Mortis," *ACL Newsletter* 22.2 (Winter 2000): 21-26.

2 Literature of the Hispanic New World holds particular promise of usefulness for modern American audiences, in view of the rising Hispanic – and hence Spanish-speaking – population in the United States and escalating U.S. contacts with countries whose language is Spanish. Cf. Edward V. George, "Latin and Spanish: Roman Culture and Hispanic America" in Richard A. LaFleur, ed., *Latin for the 21st Century* (Reading, MA: Scott Foresman - Addison Wesley, 1997), 227-36, esp. 234-35.

Various editions of the *De Orbe Novo* label the parts of the work differently. We follow the text and divisional terminology of the Complutensian 1530 edition as presented in the 1966 Graz facsimile (see bibliography, Petrus Martyr de Angleria), referring only to Decades (of which there are a total of eight) and Chapters (*capitula*) within the decades. We have exercised freedom in selecting passages, but we have not altered Martyr's words, except for deletions of words and phrases and occasional minor spelling regularizations. We have adapted punctuation. In one case (Section 1, line 3) we have added a clarifying word and have identified it by square brackets. In introducing macrons, we have generally followed Lewis and Short's *Latin Dictionary*. We have avoided assuming where macrons should occur in the names of modern era persons or places, except in handling case endings and in making vowels long where the effect will be to bring Latin pronunciation measurably closer to ordinary pronunciation in Spanish.

We acknowledge the work of the late Dr. Gareth Morgan for the concept behind the Auxiliary Sentences. We are grateful to Dr. Gary S. Elbow of the Texas Tech University Geography Faculty for his direction to important background resources; to Dr. George's Latin 2302 students at Texas Tech University, especially Bobbie Coldiron, Andrew Ha, Jeremy Jones, Sonya Jones, Erin Leedy, Chrissy Mainey, Pamela Stage, and Phuongthi Trinh, for their participation in the use of this text and for their helpful comments; to Bruce Cammack, Texas Tech Special Collections Librarian; and to the staff and personnel of the Department of Classical and Modern Languages and Literatures, the Language Learning Laboratory, and the Teaching and Learning Technology Center at Texas Tech University for technical support. We are grateful to Lou Bolchazy for support of this project, and to LeaAnn Osburn, her Bolchazy-Carducci staff colleagues, and BCP's readers for correcting errors and suggesting valuable revisions. We are ourselves responsible for any shortcomings.

Constance P. Iacona
Wayne, Pennsylvania

Edward V. George
Lubbock, Texas

December, 2001/Updated June 2005

INTRODUCTION

Peter Martyr of Angleria (1457–1526), named after a 13th century saint, was born in northern Italy. After acquiring a classical education, he spent several years in Rome, becoming an expert in ancient geography. At the age of thirty, he moved to Spain and served the Castilian court as a diplomat. When leaving for Spain, he promised that he would keep his Italian patron, Cardinal Ascanio Sforza, abreast of his experiences. Thus originated the *Decades de Orbe Novo*, a series of reports on the exploration and conquest of the "New World" (a phrase which he is credited with coining). Martyr began these reports in 1493 and brought the first of them to print in 1511.

Samuel Eliot Morison describes the *De Orbe Novo* as the earliest history of the New World. It was an important channel through which Europe outside Spain received word of early Spanish contacts across the Atlantic. Although Martyr himself never crossed the Atlantic, his insatiable curiosity drove him to interview Columbus and his shipmates, whom he met on their return to Europe, as well as other players in the events. These contacts, in addition to Martyr's readiness to handle other people's views critically, enrich the value of the work. Martyr also served as secretary to the Castilian court's Council of the Indies for several years before his death in 1526.

When these narratives were composed, the full scope of the new encounters was not yet realized. It was only gradually that the Europeans became aware that they had actually happened upon two hitherto unknown continents.

Other Sources for Columbus' First Voyage (1492–93)

The background notes, located immediately after each section of Latin text, provide context for Martyr's narrative. These notes refer the reader to the other main sources for the first voyage. Martyr does not always agree with them. The main alternate sources include:

1. Columbus' own journal of the voyage

We possess not the original, but an abstraction of it by Fray Bartolomé de Las Casas (1474–1566), a Dominican friar with a celebrated career of his own as a defender of the character and the rights of the New World natives. (See bibliography, Dunn and Kelley.)

2. Columbus' letter of 1493 announcing his discoveries

The letter was written in Spanish, but quickly translated into Latin for distribution all over Europe. (Latin served as Europe's international language.) (See bibliography, Cristoforo Colombo, 1966.)

3. The biography of Christopher Columbus by his son Ferdinand

(See bibliography, Ferdinand Columbus.)

4. Gonzalo Fernández de Oviedo's *Natural History of the West Indies*

Oviedo (1478–1557) met Columbus in 1490, and was involved in New World activities of the Spanish through a long political, military, and literary career. He wrote the *Natural History* in 1524–25, and published the first part of it in 1535. (See bibliography, Fernández de Oviedo, 1992; and for background on Oviedo see Fernández de Oviedo, 1959, edited by Stoudemire.)

Columbus: A Controversial Figure

Opinions of Columbus vary widely. Some historians emphasize his qualities as a courageous, determined pioneer. Samuel Eliot Morison shows this view in *Admiral of the Ocean Sea*. Others condemn him for his role in starting the Europeans on a career of devastation among the peoples of the New World. One of these writers is Kirkpatrick Sale, author of *The Conquest of Paradise*. Both of these books include narratives of Columbus' first voyage and can serve as backgrounds against which to place Martyr's own text.

You will note a number of places where Martyr's version of the story varies from that of Columbus. These differences may result from varying recollections of Martyr's witnesses, from Columbus' own wish to distort or truncate the story, or from a desire by Martyr to put a different spin on events.

Martyr's Latinity

When Peter Martyr was writing, there was a consensus among scholars and literary people that proper Latin was the Latin of ancient Roman writers, especially the orator and philosophical writer Marcus Tullius Cicero (106–43 BCE). Thus if you have learned the basics of classical Latin, you already know Martyr's Latin, along with that of many of his contemporaries.

Martyr's narrative style closely resembles that of Julius Caesar's *Gallic Wars*. Like Caesar, Martyr puts a premium on spare simplicity of narrative rather than ornate embellishment. This priority also makes for easier reading and quicker understanding.

The Auxiliary Sentences

The Auxiliary Sentences we provide here are simplifications of the narrative which are based on the main text. Depending on your proficiency, you may work with these sentences prior to addressing the text for each section; or, alternatively, you may proceed directly to reading the main text, and resort to the Auxiliary Sentences as needed. Experience with intermediate students shows that gradual transition from the former of these strategies to the latter often works best.

In any event, when working with the Auxiliary Sentences for any section, you will get help from the Vocabulary and Grammar Notes designated for that section, as well as the Lexicon at the end of the book.

CHRONOLOGY OF COLUMBUS' FIRST VOYAGE

Year	Date (following Columbus' *Diario*)	Events
1492	August 3	Columbus leaves port at Palos in Spain
	September 6	Columbus' departure from the Canary Islands
	October 10	Complaints among Columbus' sailors come to a head
	October 12	Land sighted: arrival at San Salvador
	October 15	Island of Santa María de la Concepción
	October 16	Island of Fernandina
	October 19	Island of Isabela
	October 28– December 5	Exploration off Cuba
	November 21	Martín Alonso Pinzón, captain of the *Pinta*, takes off on his own
	December 5– January 16	Exploration of Hispaniola
	December 12–13	The capture of a woman; they treat her well and she draws the natives to the shore. *In Martyr's narrative, this takes place after the December 25 wrecking of the Santa María (see below and Section 3 in the text).*
	December 16	They meet a lone native in a canoe; they treat him well, and he calms the natives' fears about the strangers
	December 25	The *Santa María* runs aground and wrecks off Hispaniola
	December 26	Building of the settlement of La Navidad commences near the wreck of the *Santa María*

1493	January 4	Columbus sets sail in the *Niña* from La Navidad, leaving 38 men behind
	January 6	Martín Alonso Pinzón and the *Pinta* reunite with Columbus and the *Niña*
	January 16	The *Niña* and the *Pinta* head homeward across the Atlantic
	February 18	They land on Santa María Island in the Azores, a Portuguese possession
	February 22	They leave the Azores
	March 4	They reach the Rock of Sintra, near Lisbon, Portugal
	March 15	They return to Palos

ABBREVIATIONS

References are to items in the bibliography.

Berger	Berger, Adolf, 1953.
Columbus Letter	Colombo, Cristoforo, 1966. This is the widely published 1493 Latin version of Columbus' letter on his first voyage, with translations by Frank E. Robbins, which are used here.
Diario	Dunn and Kelley, 1989. Columbus' journal, abstracted by Bartolomé de Las Casas.
Eatough	Symcox et al., 1998. Geoffrey Eatough's text, translation, and commentary for selections from Peter Martyr.
MacNutt	Peter Martyr d'Anghera, 1912. F.A. MacNutt's translation of Peter Martyr's *De Orbe Novo*.
Marx	Columbus, Christopher, 1972. *Columbus' Letter on His First Voyage.*
Morison	Morison, Samuel Eliot, 1942.
Oviedo	Fernández de Oviedo, Gonzalo, 1992.
Sale	Sale, Kirkpatrick, 1990.

VOCABULARY NOTES, LATIN TEXT, AND BACKGROUND NOTES

SECTION 1

Fig. 1. Ferdinand, King of Spain.

Vocabulary and Notes

1   **Ligur, -uris,** (adj.) of Liguria. See Fig. 2 in background notes.

1–2   **Fernandō et Helisabethae,** See Fig. 2 in background notes.

3   **suādeō, suadēre, suāsī,** to persuade (+ dat.); *here,* with indirect statement; with *ut* and a subjunctive verb in Classical Latin

      ab occidente nostrō, from our west (**occidens, -entis,** m.), instead of sailing from the east

4   **inventūrum** = *inventūrum esse*

      nāvigium, -ī, n. vessel

5   **attineō, attinēre, attinuī, attentum,** to pertain, to be pertinent; modifying *rebus*

      instruō, instruere, instrūxī, instructum, to equip, to outfit (+ acc. and abl.)

6   **augeō, augēre, auxī, auctum,** to spread, to increase

      margarīta, -ae, f. pearl

7   **arōma, arōmatis,** n. spice

      inopīnātus, -a, -um, (adj.) unexpected, unanticipated

8   **instō, instāre, institī, instātum,** to press, insist, demand. **Instantī** = dative singular masculine, present participle with the pronoun "to him" understood

      rēgius, -a, -um, (adj.) royal

      fiscus, -ī, m. treasury

      destinō, destināre, destināvī, destinātum, to allocate

9   **onerārius, -a, -um,** (adj.) for cargo

      ūnum onerārium The *Santa María* was a cargo ship. See background notes.

      mercātōrius, -a, -um, (adj.) for merchant trade

10   **caravella, -ae,** f. caravel

11   **circiter,** (adv.) nearly, approximately

      Kal. = *Kalendās;* the Calends, the first day of the month

12   **Septembrīs** = *Septembrēs,* (adj.) of September

      nōnāgēsimus, -a, -um, (adj.) ninetieth

13   **quadringentēsimus, -a, -um,** (adj.) four hundreth

      millēsimus, -a, -um, (adj.) one thousandth

      ā nostrā salūte = "from [the year of] our salvation," i.e. from the date of the birth of Christ

14   **instituō, instituere, instituī, institūtum,** to put together, to organize

      cum virīs Hispānīs circiter CCXX Martyr says there were 220 men. See background notes.

1. Columbus Obtains Royal Spanish Support and Sets Out

Columbus successfully proposed his plan to Ferdinand, King of Aragon and Isabella, Queen of Castile. They provided funds for three ships (the *Santa María*, the *Niña*, and the *Pinta*) and in January of 1492 commanded Columbus to go to India with this fleet. The author of this narrative, Peter Martyr, says there were 220 men and does not discuss the departure from the mainland at Palos, Spain, on August 3. He actually refers here to when the fleet set sail from the Canary Islands, a Spanish possession in the Atlantic, on September 6.

    Christophorus Colōnus, Ligur vir, Fernandō et
    Helisabethae Rēgibus Catholicīs prōposuit et
    suāsit sē ab occidente nostrō fīnitimās Indiae
    insulās inventūrum, sī [eum] nāvigiīs et rēbus ad
5   nāvigātiōnem attinentibus instruerent, ā quibus
    augērī Christiāna religiō, et margarītārum
    arōmatumque et aurī inopīnāta cōpia habērī
    facile posset. Instantī ex rēgiō fiscō destināta sunt
    tria nāvigia, ūnum onerārium, alia duo mercātōria
10   levia, quae ab Hispānīs caravellae vocantur.
    Hīs habitīs, ab Hispānīs lītoribus circiter Kal.
    Septembrīs annī secundī et nōnāgēsimī suprā
    quadringentēsimum et millēsimum ā nostrā salūte,
    iter institūtum cum virīs Hispānīs circiter CCXX
15   Colōnus coepit.

Background Notes

1. Columbus Obtains Royal Spanish Support and Sets Out

          Christophorus Colōnus, Ligur vir, Fernandō et
          Helisabethae Rēgibus Catholicīs prōposuit et
          suāsit sē ab occidente nostrō fīnitimās Indiae
          insulās inventūrum, sī [eum] nāvigiīs et rēbus ad
   5   nāvigātiōnem attinentibus instruerent, ā quibus
          augērī Christiāna religiō, et margarītārum
          arōmatumque et aurī inopīnāta cōpia habērī
          facile posset. Instantī ex rēgiō fiscō destināta sunt
          tria nāvigia, ūnum onerārium, alia duo mercātōria
   10   levia, quae ab Hispānīs caravellae vocantur.
          Hīs habitīs, ab Hispānīs lītoribus circiter Kal.
          Septembrīs annī secundī et nōnāgēsimī suprā
          quadringentēsimum et millēsimum ā nostrā salūte,
          iter īnstitūtum cum virīs Hispānīs circiter CCXX
   15   Colōnus coepit.

9   **ūnum onerārium** The *Santa María,*   14   **cum virīs Hispānīs circiter CCXX**
     in contrast to the *Niña* and the   Martyr says there were 220 men.
     Pinta, was a cargo ship; caravels   Most sources say the fleet was
     are smaller, lighter, and faster.   composed of 90 men, but Oviedo
                                                         says there were 120.

Latin Form	Identification	Equivalent
Christophorus Colōnus	Christopher Columbus	Cristóbal Colón
Cuba, Cubae, f.	Cuba, the island	Cuba
Fernandus, Fernandī, m.	Ferdinand, King of Aragon, 1479–1516	Fernando
Grānātensēs Hispānī	inhabitants of Andalusia in Spain	"Andalusians" (MacNutt)
Guaccanarillus, Guaccanarillī, m.	the Taino[3] king met by Columbus on his first voyage	Gaucanagarí
Helisabetha, Helisabethae, f.	Isabel, Queen of Castile and León, 1474–1504	Isabella
Hispaniola, Hispaniolae, f.	the island comprising Haiti and the Dominican Republic	Hispaniola
Ioanna, Ioannae, f.	name given to Cuba	Cuba
Insubrēs, Insubrium, m.pl.	ancient inhabitants of northern Italy	"Milanese" (MacNutt)
Ligur, Liguris, (adj.)	Ligurian, of the area of Genoa, Italy	Ligurian

Fig. 2. Correlation of Latin, English, and Spanish Names.

3 Taino: The name of the Caribbean inhabitants first met by Columbus.

Fig. 3. Spanish Vessel.

Vocabulary and Notes

1   **occidō, occidere, occidī, occāsum,** to set, sink down

2   **secūtus** perfect passive participle of **sequor, sequī, secūtus sum,** to follow

licet, *here,* "although" (with subjunctive)

laevus –a -um, the left (i.e. south, to a voyager traveling west)

paulisper, "for a little while," "for a short time"

licet in laevam paulisper, i.e. to the left (the south) a little bit.

3   **coelō** = *caelō*

tantum, (adv.) only

4   **contentus, -a, -um,** (adj.) content. With ablative (*coelō, aquā*). Another possible meaning: "surrounded," as the perfect passive participle of *contineō.*

comes, comitis, m./f. companion, fellow traveler

murmurō, murmurāre, murmurāvī, murmurātum, to grumble. See background notes for further explanation of the developing hostility.

5   **tacitē,** adverb from **tacitus, -a, -um,** (adj.) silent

convīcium, -ī, n. insult, abuse

6   **urgeō, urgēre, ursī,** to encourage

urgēre, cogitāre: historical infinitives. Subject = the ships' crews.

perimō, perimere, perēmī, peremptum, to kill. *dē perimendō* = "about killing [him]." Gerund.

dēmum, (adv.) finally

vel, (adv.) even

7   **prōiiciendō** Understand "him" as the object.

consulēbātur "Consultation was taken." Impersonal.

trīcēsimus, -a, -um, (adj.) thirtieth

8   **perciēō, perciēre, percīvī, percītum,** to stir up, to excite

prōclāmō, prōclāmāre, prōclāmāvī, prōclāmātum, to insist, cry out

9   **ulterius,** (comparative adv.) any further. *nē ulterius prōcēderet* = jussive subjunctive clause, dependent on *stimulābant hominem.*

stimulō, stimulāre, stimulāvī, stimulātum, to urge

hominem = Columbus

10   **blandus, -a, -um,** (adj.) soft, soothing

modo ... modo ... "first ... then ..."

11   **īrātōs:** Adjective used substantively with "men" understood.

mulceō, mulcēre, mulsī, mulsum, to soothe, stroke

dēpascō, dēpascere, dēpāvī, dēpastum, to feed (e.g. one's hopes)

12   **optātum:** perfect passive participle modifying *prospectum*

Optātum . . . suscipiunt: October 11–12. This first landfall is widely believed to be Watling Island in the Bahamas. See the map of the Caribbean on p.12

prospectus, -ūs, m. sight

suscipiō, suscipere, suscēpī, susceptum, to receive, to absorb, to catch

13   **patefaciō, patefacere, patefēcī, patefactum,** to expose, to bring to light

sex tantum insulās See background notes for more information about these six islands.

tantum, (adv.) only

14   **iīs** = *eīs*

15   **alteram Hispāniolam . . . alteram Ioannam,** the one Hispaniola . . . the other Cuba. See background notes for more information about Hispaniola and Cuba.

16   **pro certō habēre** = to regard as certain

2. The Ocean Voyage:
A Restless Crew, Then Land is Sighted

Leaving the Canary Islands, the ships headed westward. On October 7, near the end of the voyage, the Spaniards saw birds fly to the southwest and guessed that there was land in that direction. Columbus changed course accordingly (*Diario*, p. 55, for October 7) and kept heading that way until October 11. Columbus also had to deal with a grumbling crew. The crisis passed, and the expedition reached the New World.

Ab hīs igitur insulīs Colōnus, occidentem sōlem
semper secūtus, licet in laevam paulisper, trēs
et trīgintā continuōs diēs, coelō tantum et aquā
contentus, nāvigāvit. Hispānī comitēs murmurāre
5   prīmum tacitē coepērunt. Mox apertīs convīciīs
urgēre, dē perimendō cōgitāre, dēmum vel in mare
prōiiciendō consulēbātur. Post trīcēsimum iam
diem fūrōre percītī prōclāmābant ut redūcerentur;
nē ulterius prōcēderet stimulābant hominem. Ipse
10   vērō blandīs modo verbīs, amplā spē modo, diem
ex diē prōtrahens, īrātōs mulcēbat, dēpascēbat.
Optātum tandem terrae prospectum laetī suscipiunt.
Patefēcit nāvigātiōne hāc prīmā sex tantum insulās,
atque ex iīs duās inaudītae magnitūdinis, quārum
15   alteram Hispāniolam, Ioannam alteram vocāvit, sed
Ioannam esse insulam nōn prō certō habuit.

Background Notes

2. The Ocean Voyage: A Restless Crew, Then Land is Sighted

Ab hīs igitur insulīs Colōnus, occidentem sōlem
semper secūtus, licet in laevam paulisper, trēs
et trīgintā continuōs diēs, coelō tantum et aquā
contentus, nāvigāvit. Hispānī comitēs murmurāre
5   prīmum tacitē coepērunt. Mox apertīs convīciīs
urgēre, dē perimendō cōgitāre, dēmum vel in mare
prōiiciendō cōnsulēbātur. Post trīcēsimum iam
diem furōre percītī prōclāmābant ut redūcerentur;
nē ulterius prōcēderet stimulābant hominem. Ipse
10   vērō blandīs modo verbīs, amplā spē modo, diem
ex diē prōtrahens, īrātōs mulcēbat, dēpascēbat.
Optātum tandem terrae prospectum laetī suscipiunt.
Patefēcit nāvigātiōne hāc prīmā sex tantum insulās,
atque ex iīs duās inaudītae magnitūdinis, quārum
15   alteram Hispāniolam, Ioannam alteram vocāvit, sed
Ioannam esse insulam nōn prō certō habuit.

**4–5 Hispānī comitēs murmurāre prī-
mum tacitē coepērunt.** *Diario*
Oct. 10 (p. 57): "Here the men
could no longer stand it; they com-
plained of the long voyage. But the
Admiral encouraged them as best
he could, giving them good hope
of the benefits that they would be
able to secure. And he added that
it was useless to complain since
he had come to find the Indies
and thus had to continue the voyage until he found them, with the
help of our Lord." The *Diario* is
even stronger in an entry for Feb.
14, 1493, looking back: "[God]
had delivered him on the outward
voyage, when he had greater rea-
son to fear from his troubles with
the sailors and people that he
took with him, who all, with one
voice, were determined to go back
and to rise against him in protest.
And the eternal God gave him
strength and resolution against
all of them" (*Diario*, p. 369).
Oviedo (pp. 24–25) and Las Casas (1951, pp. 186-90), more like
Martyr, describe gradually developing hostility over a longer time.

Both of them tell of the threats to
throw Columbus overboard. They
also describe a last minute com-
promise by Columbus; just before
the arrival at San Salvador, they
say, he agrees with the sailors that
he will turn around if they have
not found land in three days. This
claim disagrees with the unyield-
ing position Columbus takes in
the *Diario*.

13   sex tantum insulās Martyr writes
of the six islands that Columbus
saw on his first voyage, but Columbus attests to having seen
numerous islands: "I reached the
Indian Sea, there I found very
many islands, inhabited by numberless people" (Columbus Letter, p. 8). The letter then *names*
six islands. See figure 4.

In the *Diario* for Oct. 14 (p. 77), he
says, "I saw so many islands that I
did not know how to decide which
one I would go to first. And those
men whom I had taken [referring
to captured natives] told me by
signs that they were so very many
that they were numberless. And

they named by their names more than a hundred." Perhaps Martyr intends simply to condense his narrative by focusing on the six highlighted islands, but even at that, his assertion is puzzling.

14–16 duās inaudītae magnitūdinis, quārum alteram Hispāniolam, Ioannam alteram vocāvit, sed Ioannam esse insulam nōn prō certō habuit Hispaniola is the island which now comprises Haiti and the Dominican Republic. *Ioanna* means Cuba, named by Columbus after the Infante Don Juan (died 1497), heir to the Castilian crown, son of Ferdinand and Isabella. See Fig. 2. Although Columbus estimates the size of Cuba as an island, he also says, "when we first put in [there], I . . . found it so large . . . that I believed it to be no island, but the continental province of Cathay [i.e. China]" (Columbus Letter, p. 8). Columbus overestimated the size of Cuba, which he claimed was larger than England and Scotland combined. He also exaggerated the circumference of Hispaniola (Columbus Letter, p.14). However, the Columbus Letter also asserts (p. 9) that he learned from the natives "that this province was in fact an island." And in the *Diario* entry for Nov. 2 (p. 131) he "still affirms that the island [of Cuba] is *tierra firme* [the Spanish expression for 'mainland']." Eatough says that "Martyr resisted Columbus' persistent continental claims for the island" (p. 225).

Islands Named in Columbus' 1493 Letter	Date of Arrival (all 1492)	Modern Identification (Morison, 1942)
San Salvador	Oct. 12	Watling Island, Bahamas
Santa María de la Concepción	Oct. 15	Rum Cay, Bahamas
Fernandina	Oct. 16	Long Island, Bahamas
Isabela	Oct. 19	Crooked Island, Bahamas
Juana	Oct. 28	Cuba (native name "Colba": *Diario*, p. 109, for Oct. 21)
Hispana	Dec. 5	Hispaniola

Fig. 4. Correlation of Columbus' Identification of Islands with their Modern Names.

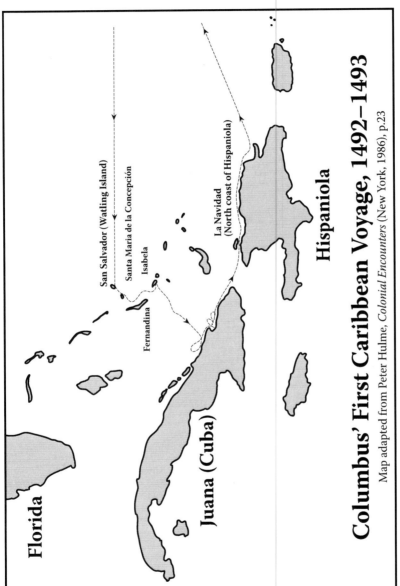

Florida

Juana (Cuba)

San Salvador (Watling Island)

Santa Maria de la Concepción

Isabela

Fernandina

La Navidad
(North coast of Hispaniola)

Hispaniola

Columbus' First Caribbean Voyage, 1492–1493

Map adapted from Peter Hulme, *Colonial Encounters* (New York, 1986), p.23

Map of the Caribbean

Fig. 5 The Spaniards Sight the Islands.

Vocabulary and Notes

1   **ēgredior, ēgredī, ēgressus sum,** to disembark, to land. The participle modifies the subject.

    indigena, -ae, m./f. inhabitant, native

1–2   **Ibi prīmum ad terram ēgressī hominēs indigenās vīdērunt** Actually, the Spanish had already met the natives weeks earlier. See background notes.

2   **conspicor, conspicārī, conspicātus sum,** to catch sight of

3   **agmen, -inis,** n. a moving throng; a mass of people on the move. *facto agmine* – ablative absolute.

    condensus, -a, -um, (adj.) dense

    nemus, -oris, n. grove, woods

3–4   **velutī ā canibus Gallicīs timidī leporēs** See background notes for appropriateness of the simile.

4   **lepus, -oris,** m. hare

    sēsē = *sē*

    sē recipere, to retreat to, to escape to, to take refuge in (with *in* or *ad* + acc.)

    nostrī = "our men." As often in Martyr's narrative.

5   **insequor, insequī, insecūtus sum,** to follow; modifying the subject *nostrī.*

    tantum, (adv.) only

6   **hanc** = *hanc mulierem*

7   **saturō, saturāre, saturāvī, saturātum,** to fill

7–9   **ea gens omnis . . . nūda penitus vītam dūcit, nātūrā contenta** Here and elsewhere Martyr connects the nakedness of the natives with the virtuous simplicity of their life.

8   **penitus,** (adv.) completely, entirely

9   **contentus, -a, -um,** (adj.) content. *nātūrā contenta* = "content with their natural state."

solvō, solvere, solvī, solūtum, to release, to liberate

quam prīmum = "as soon as"

10   **concēdō, concēdere, concessī, concessum,** to go away

    quō, (adv.) whither, to where

11   **dīvertō, dīvertere, dīvertī, dīversum,** to scatter

12   **ornātus, -ūs,** m. attire, garb

    līberālitās, līberālitātis, f. generosity, gift

    certātim, (adv.) in competition (with each other)

13   **coelō** = *caelō*

    autumō, autumāre, autumāvī, autumātum, to affirm

15   **honōrificē,** (adv.) with honor

    occāsus, occāsūs, m. setting (of the sun)

    vergō, vergere, to incline, to turn; *here,* to sink

15–17   **nostrīs . . . flectentibus:** ablative absolute.

16   **salūtātiōnis angelicae** = "of the angelic greeting:" a traditional Catholic prayer. See background notes.

    genū, -ūs, n. knee

    rītus, -ūs, m. rite, ritual

17   **flectō, flectere, flexī, flexum,** to bend

    itidem, (adv.) likewise

    crux, crucis, f. the Christian cross

    quīcumque, quaecumque, quodcumque, (pronoun) whoever, whatever

18   **colō, colere, coluī, cultum,** to venerate, to pay honor to

    adōrō, adōrāre, adōrāvī, adōrātum, to adore

3. The Encounter with the New World Inhabitants

Columbus spent several weeks scouting along the coast of Cuba (October 28–December 5). During that time, on November 21, Martín Alonso Pinzón, captain of the *Pinta*, defied Columbus and took off on his own, thinking that the gold sought by the Spanish could be found elsewhere. On December 5, Columbus headed for Hispaniola in the *Niña* and the *Santa María*. A few days later the Spanish succeeded in capturing a native woman on the Hispaniola coast. This episode, described below, is told at greater length in the *Diario*, pp. 219–225, for December 12 and 13.

    Ibi prīmum ad terram ēgressī hominēs indigenās
    vīdērunt, quī venientem inaudītam gentem conspicātī,
    factō agmine in condensa nemora omnēs, velutī ā canibus
    Gallicīs timidī leporēs, sēsē fugientēs recipiunt. Nostrī,
5   multitūdinem insecūtī, mulierem tantum capiunt.
    Hanc cum ad nāvēs perdūxissent, nostrīs cibīs et vīnō
    bene saturātam atque ornātam vestibus (nam ea gens
    omnis utriusque sexūs nūda penitus vītam dūcit, nātūrā
    contenta), solūtam relīquērunt. Quam prīmum ad
10   suōs mulier concessit (sciēbat enim illa quō fugientēs
    dīverterent), ostendissetque mīrum esse nostrōrum
    ornātum et līberālitātem, omnēs ad lītora certātim
    concurrunt; gentem esse missam ē coelō autumant. Ē
    nāvibus dēscendentēs nostrī ā rēge et reliquīs indigenīs
15   honōrificē recipiuntur. Sōle ad occāsum vergente, nostrīs,
    datō salūtātiōnis angelicae signō, genua Christiānō rītū
    flectentibus, itidem illī faciēbant. Crucem, quōcumque
    modō Christiānōs colere conspicerent, adōrābant.

Background Notes

3. The Encounter with the New World Inhabitants

Ibi prīmum ad terram ēgressī hominēs indigenās
vīdērunt, quī venientem inaudītam gentem conspicātī,
factō agmine in condensa nemora omnēs, velutī ā canibus
Gallicīs timidī leporēs, sēsē fugientēs recipiunt. Nostrī,
5   multitūdinem insecūtī, mulierem tantum capiunt.
Hanc cum ad nāvēs perdūxissent, nostrīs cibīs et vīnō
bene saturātam atque ornātam vestibus (nam ea gens
omnis utriusque sexūs nūda penitus vītam dūcit, nātūrā
contenta), solūtam relīquērunt. Quam prīmum ad
10   suōs mulier concessit (sciēbat enim illa quō fugientēs
dīverterent), ostendissetque mīrum esse nostrōrum
ornātum et līberālitātem, omnēs ad lītora certātim
concurrunt; gentem esse missam ē coelō autumant.
Ē nāvibus dēscendentēs nostrī ā rēge et reliquīs indigenīs
15   honōrificē recipiuntur. Sōle ad occāsum vergente, nostrīs,
datō salūtātiōnis angelicae signō, genua Christiānō rītū
flectentibus, itidem illī faciēbant. Crucem, quōcumque
modō Christiānōs colere conspicerent, adōrābant.

1–2   Ibi prīmum ad terram ēgressī hominēs indigenās vīdērunt.
Eatough explains Martyr's narrative by calling the encounters on Hispaniola "the first *serious* encounters" (p. 227: emphasis added). In the Columbus Letter, Columbus acknowledges, with remarkable frankness, "As soon as I came to that sea I forcibly seized some Indians from the first island [presumably San Salvador] so that they might learn from us and similarly teach us the things of which they had knowledge in those parts" (p. 12). During his exploration of the Cuban coast before arrival at Hispaniola, he notes, "I had already learned from some Indians whom I had taken aboard . . . that this province was in fact an island" (p. 9).

3–4   velutī ā canibus Gallicīs timidī leporēs Eatough notes (p. 227) the appropriateness of the simile in view of the Spaniards' use, from the second voyage onward, of dogs to attack or frighten the natives.

16   salūtātiōnis angelicae "The angelic greeting" is the traditional Catholic prayer called the *Angelus*, commemorating the angel Gabriel's greeting to Mary. It was prayed three times daily.

On Cannibals

A few lines after the encounter with the New World inhabitants, Martyr says that the Spaniards "learned by hearsay that not far from those islands are the islands of wild men they called Caribs, who feed on human flesh." (Translated by Eatough, p. 46. From "Carib" we get the words "Caribbean" and "cannibal.") He describes in detail the natives' stories of how the cannibals process human bodies. The *Diario* (e.g. p. 167 for November 23; p. 339 for January 15) also cites stories of cannibals whom Las Casas says Columbus heard about from the natives Columbus met. In neither case is there a report that Columbus and his men *directly* observed cannibal activity. There have been various views of the occurrence and activity of cannibals in the Caribbean at the time of Columbus' arrival. Peter Hulme, *Colonial Encounters: Europe and the Native Caribbean, 1492–1797*, Chapter 1, "Columbus and the Cannibals" and Kirkpatrick Sale, *The Conquest of Paradise* (cf. pp. 129–35), argue that there is no reliable evidence to support Martyr's description of cannibal activity here. The Spaniards had a stake in claiming whenever possible that the natives were cannibals. The charge of cannibalism, a hideous crime in European eyes, was justification for unrestrained warfare against the peoples the Spanish met.

Fig. 6. Natives Watch the Spaniards Arriving.

Vocabulary and Notes

1   quīdam, quaedam, quoddam, (adj.) a certain; a kind of, what one might call

panicum, -ī, n. Italian millet, *here*, used as an adjective. See background notes.

2   Insubrēs, -ium, m./f. pl. Insubrians: inhabitants of the region around Milan, Italy. See Fig. 2.

Grānātensēs Hispani: people of Granada, the Andalusians. See Fig. 2.

3   discrīmen, -inis, n. difference

panicula, -ae, f. head, ear

3–4   Et huius panicula ... crassitūdine Verb omitted in this sentence. Supply *est*.

4   spitama, -ae, f. a length just under 9 inches; *here*, used as an ablative of degree of difference.

in acūtum = "to a point"

lacertus, -ī, m. upper arm

ferē, (adv.) approximately

crassitūdō, -tūdinis, f. thickness

5   configō, configere, confixī, confixum, to fasten, to join together.

6   pīsum legūmen, pīsī legūminis, n. pea

aemulor, aemulārī, aemulātus sum, to imitate, be like

albeō, albēre, to be white

acerbus, -a, -um, (adj.) *here* = "immature," "still growing"

7   mātūrescō, mātūrescere, mātūruī, to mature, to become ripe

efficiō, efficere, effēcī, effectum, to make, to form, to complete

candor, -ōris, m. whiteness

8   nix, nivis, f. snow

exsuperō, exsuperāre, exsuperāvī, exsuperātum, to surpass. (= *superō*)

maizium, -ī, n. maizei See background notes.

9   aurum See background notes for more information.

aliquī, aliqua, aliquod, (adj.) some

aestimātiō, aestimātiōnis, f. value

10   auricula, -ae, f. ear

torulus, -ī, n. *here*, lobe (of the ear)

nāris, -is, f. nostril; pl., nose

inferciō, infercīre, infersī, infertum, to insert, to stuff

10–11   in tenuissimās dīductum lāminās See background notes.

11   dīdūcō, dīdūcere, dīdūxī, dīductum, to draw out, spread

lāmina, -ae, f. sheet

ferunt: *here*, "they wear"; understand "gold (it)" as the object with *infertum* and *dīductum* modifying it.

12   eōs = the Taino (the proper name for the island natives)

commeō, commeāre, commeāvī, commeātum, to come and go, to travel. *Commeāre* and *noscere* are both infinitives in indirect statement depending on *nostrī didicissent*.

ipsōs = the Taino

13–16   quaerere ab eīs per signa ... neque magnō labōre lectum See the background notes.

13   discō, discere, didicī, to learn, to find out

14   unde = from where

sibi = for themselves

comparō, comparāre, comparāvī, comparātum, to procure

14–15   Quantum ... licuit = "As far as it was permitted," "as far as it was possible"

15   arēna, -ae, f. sand

15–16   ex fluviōrum ... labōre lectum. Supply *comparātum esse compererunt*, ("they learned that it was procured,"); also supply *esse* with *lectum*; *collābentibus* modifies *arēnīs*

16   collābor, collābī, collapsum, to come tumbling down

legō, legere, lēgī, lectum, to collect, to gather

4. Strange Plants and Gold Ornaments

Farther down the coast of Hispaniola, the Spaniards sighted an Indian in a canoe. They treated him well, and when he pulled into shore he gave a favorable report of the visitors. The Spaniards met several hundred natives, among them a young king with an old tutor and other advisors (*Diario*, pp. 231–233). The cacique (i.e. king: pronounced "kah-sée-kay") Guacanagarí (Guaccanarillus in Latin, see Fig. 2.) reportedly said he could show Columbus where the Spanish might easily obtain gold on the island, and also named other islands where gold was accessible (*Diario*, p. 286). The natives, believing the Spaniards had come from the heavens, treated them kindly and generously. Columbus writes (*Diario*, pp. 235–237) to Ferdinand and Isabella that this island as well as the others now belongs to Castile. He continues that the natives are so cowardly that they would not fight against even three men and that thus they can be ordered to plant, build towns, and do whatever is needed. In this passage, Peter Martyr describes a grain previously unknown to Europeans, and the Spaniards see gold.

> Pānem ex frūmentō quōdam pānicō, cuius est apud
> Insubrēs et Grānātensēs Hispānōs maxima cōpia, nōn
> magnō discrīmine conficiunt. Et huius pānicula longior
> spitamā in acūtum tendens, lacertī ferē crassitūdine.
> 5   Grāna mīrō ordine ā nātūrā confixa. Formā et corpore
> pīsum legūmen aemulantur. Albent acerba; ubi
> mātūruērunt, nigerrima efficiuntur; fracta, candōre
> nivem exsuperant. Maizium id frūmentī genus appellant.
>
> Et est apud eōs aurum alicuius aestimātiōnis, nam
> 10   auriculārum torulīs et nāribus perforātīs infertum in
> tenuissimās dīductum lāminās ferunt. Cum tamen neque
> ad eōs commeāre mercātōrēs, nec ipsōs alia lītora noscere
> praeter sua nostrī didicissent, quaerere ab eīs per signa
> coepērunt, unde sibi id aurum comparārent. Quantum
> 15   signīs colligere licuit, ex fluviōrum arēnīs ab altīs
> montibus collābentibus id, neque magnō labōre lectum.

Background Notes

4. Strange Plants and Gold Ornaments

Pānem ex frūmentō quōdam pānicō, cuius est apud
Insubrēs et Grānātensēs Hispānōs maxima cōpia, nōn
magnō discrīmine conficiunt. Et huius pānicula longior
spitamā in acūtum tendens, lacertī ferē crassitūdine.
5   Grāna mīrō ordine ā nātūrā confixa. Formā et corpore
pīsum legūmen aemulantur. Albent acerba; ubi
mātūruērunt, nigerrima efficiuntur; fracta, candōre
nivem exsuperant. Maizium id frūmentī genus appellant.

Et est apud eōs aurum alicuius aestimātiōnis, nam
10   auriculārum torulīs et nāribus perforātīs infertum in
tenuissimās dīductum lāminās ferunt. Cum tamen neque
ad eōs commeāre mercātōrēs, nec ipsōs alia lītora noscere
praeter sua nostrī didicissent, quaerere ab eīs per signa
coepērunt, unde sibi id aurum comparārent. Quantum
15   signīs colligere licuit, ex fluviōrum arēnīs ab altīs
montibus collābentibus id, neque magnō labōre lectum.

1   **pānicum** Italian millet, *setaria Italica*. Also known as "panic-grass." Martyr apparently uses the word as an adjective, *pānicus*, modifying *frūmentō*. Martyr seems to be using *pānicum* to refer more to a bread-making grain than to the various kinds of plants we identify as millet today. (The Italian millet or *setaria* is commonly known as foxtail, and the *miliaceum* is noted as "broomcorn" and used as birdseed in America.) Similarly, the Spanish used *panizo* for the cereal grains wheat, millet, barley, and oats, as the British use "corn" for grain.

4   **spitama** a measure of length or span just under 9 inches, c. 224 mm. (spelled *spithama* in the *Oxford Latin Dictionary*).

8   **maizium** Here Martyr "gives us the first extended description of maize, and also its native name" (Eatough, p. 236).

9   **aurum** In all the sources Columbus repeatedly inquires about gold and keeps moving from island to island in search of the metal or other valuable resources. Note all the quick jumps from place to place in fig. 4 on p. 11.

10–11 **in tenuissimās dīductum lāminās** Note the similarity to the *Diario*, p. 237, for December 17: "He [Columbus] again sent certain Christians to the village; and in exchange for small glass beads they traded for some pieces of gold worked into thin sheets."

13–16 **quaerere ab eīs per signa . . . neque magnō labōre lectum** The cacique Guacanagarí reportedly said he could show Columbus where the Spanish might easily obtain gold on the island, and also named other islands where gold was accessible (See *Diario*, p. 286, for December 26). Thus the *Diario* implies that the Hispaniolans *do* have familiarity with people on other islands, despite Martyr's assertions to the contrary in this section of his narrative.

Fig. 7. The Spanish Build a Settlement at Navidad.

Vocabulary and Notes

1 **Hīs:** modifies *signīs.* Ablative after *contentus*

   tellūs, -ūris, f. land

1–2 **Hīs igitur . . . signīs contentus** See background notes.

2 **flō, flāre, flāvī, flātum,** to blow

3 **Zephyrus, -ī,** m. west wind

   vēr, vēris, n. spring

   propter vēr propinquum See background notes.

4–5 **Octo et trīgintā virōs . . . relīquit** See background notes.

5 **quī . . . inquīrerent** Relative clause of purpose; take *quī* as subject of *inquīrerent* and *nātūram* as its object; *inquīrerent* here means "inquire into."

   temporum: *here,* apparently, "climates." MacNutt translates *locōrum et temporum nātūram* loosely as "the country and its condition."

6 **dōnec,** (conj. foll. by subjv.) until

7 **incola, -ae,** m./f. inhabitant

   dīcēbātur = "was called"

   Guaccanarillus, -i, m. Guacanagarí, the native king. See Fig. 2.

   iciō (icō), icere, īcī, ictum, to strike. *foedus icere* = "to conclude a treaty."

7–8 **ictō . . . foedere;** an unusual ablative absolute, in the relative clause starting *cum quo.*

8 **tūtēla, -ae,** f. protection

9 **relinquēbat:** assumes Columbus as subject

   quibus potuit modīs = *quibus modīs potuit.*

   ēgit = "he acted," "he took measures"

10 **contingō, contingere, contigī, contactus,** to touch

   ergā, (prep. w. acc.) toward

   quod = "because"

11 **dēserō, dēserere, dēseruī, dēsertum,** to desert

   effundō, effundere, effūdī, effūsum, to pour out, to shed

12 **pollicitus** = *pollicitus est*

   alter . . . alterum: one person . . . another

   complector, complectī, complexus sum, to embrace. *complexi* = *complexi sunt*

13 **vēlum, -ī,** n. sail. *vēla dare* = "to set sail"

   vēla darī imperat See background notes.

14 **decem virōs . . . abdūxit** See background notes.

15 **nostrīs litterīs Latīnīs** See background notes.

16 **discrīmen, -inis,** n. difference, difficulty

   comperiō, comperīre, comperī, compertum, to learn. *compertum est:* impersonal passive.

17 **coelum** = *caelum*

17–18 **turei, boa, cauni, tayno, mayani** Taino, not Latin words; Latin meanings given in the text

18 **tayno** Taino is the name now conventionally given to the people met by Columbus.

   -ve (on *reliquave*) here = "and"

   vocābulum, -ī, n. word

19 **liquidē,** (adv.) clearly. *nōn minus liquidē . . . atque* = "not less clearly than"

   Latīnā nostrā: Add "*linguā.*"

5. The Spaniards Push Off for Home in January, 1493

On Christmas Eve, while Columbus was sleeping, the *Santa María* ran aground, not far from the town of King Cuacanagarí. (See the chronology, p. xii, for December 12–13.) After the natives helped the Spaniards unload the ship, Columbus used the timbers of the foundered ship and other materials to build a fort as the center of a colony, named "La Navidad" ("Christmas Town"), where he would later leave a detachment of thirty-eight or thirty-nine sailors behind when he sailed for home. Peter Martyr narrates the natives' stories of nearby cannibals (see background notes to section 3, p. 17), says that little is known about the natives' religion, and discusses some of the flora and fauna of Hispaniola. Martyr then describes various birds, especially parrots, and also plants, with attention to cotton. On January 4, 1493, the Spaniards departed from La Navidad in the *Niña*. When Columbus left La Navidad, he was anticipating a homeward voyage with only one ship. But on January 6, Martín Alonso Pinzón and the *Pinta* rejoined him. Ten days later, after further exploration, the two caravels (minus the wrecked *Santa María*) headed out into the Atlantic, reaching the Azores Islands February 18, stopping in Portugal, and finally coming home to port in Palos, Spain on March 15, 1493.

His igitur inventae novae tellūris et inaudītī alterīus
terrārum orbis signīs contentus, prosperō reditū flantibus
Zephyrīs, propter vēr propinquum redīre constituit.
Octo et trīginta virōs apud eum rēgem dē quō suprā
5   memorāvimus relīquit, quī locōrum et temporum
nātūram, dōnec ipse reverterētur, inquīrerent. Is rex
ab incolīs dīcēbātur Guaccanarillus, cum quō ictō
singulāris amīcitiae foedere; dē vītā et salūte ac tūtēlā
eōrum, quōs ibi relinquēbat, quibus potuit modīs, ēgit.
10   Misericordiā contactus rex ergā nostrōs, quod aliēnīs
terrīs dēsererentur, lacrimās effūdisse vīsus est, atque
omnem opem pollicitus. Sīc alter alterum complexī. Ad
Hispāniam Colōnus reditūrus vēla darī imperat, sēcum
decem virōs ex illīs abdūxit, ā quibus posse omnium
15   illārum insulārum linguam nostrīs litterīs Latīnīs sine
ullō discrīmine scrībī compertum est. Vocant enim
coelum *turei*. Domum *boa*. Aurum *cauni*. Virum bonum
tayno. Nihil *mayani*. Reliquave omnia vocābula nōn minus
liquidē prōferunt atque nōs, Latīnā nostrā.

Background Notes

5. The Spaniards Push Off for Home in January, 1493

His igitur inventae novae tellūris et inaudītī alterīus
terrārum orbis signīs contentus, prosperō reditū flantibus
Zephyrīs, propter vēr propinquum redīre constituit.
Octo et trīginta virōs apud eum rēgem dē quō suprā
5   memorāvimus relīquit, quī locōrum et temporum
nātūram, dōnec ipse reverterētur, inquīrerent. Is rex
ab incolīs dīcēbātur Guaccanarillus, cum quō ictō
singulāris amīcitiae foedere; dē vītā et salūte ac tūtēlā
eōrum, quōs ibi relinquēbat, quibus potuit modīs, ēgit.
10 Misericordiā contactus rex ergā nostrōs, quod aliēnīs
terrīs dēsererentur, lacrimās effūdisse vīsus est, atque
omnem opem pollicitus. Sīc alter alterum complexī. Ad
Hispāniam Colōnus reditūrus vēla darī imperat, sēcum
decem virōs ex illīs abdūxit, ā quibus posse omnium
15 illārum insulārum linguam nostrīs litterīs Latīnīs sine
ullō discrīmine scrībī compertum est. Vocant enim
coelum *turei.* Domum *boa.* Aurum *cauni.* Virum bonum
tayno. Nihil *mayani.* Reliquave omnia vocābula nōn minus
liquidē prōferunt atque nōs, Latīnā nostrā.

1–2   **His igitur ... inaudītī alterīus ter-**
rārum orbis ... signīs contentus
MacNutt refers to "a hitherto unknown continent," while Eatough
calls it "this other world unheard
of before." The expression "circle of lands" is transferred from
the European/African "circle of
lands" centered on the Mediter-
ranean Sea. "Martyr may have
thought it was a new world, but
Columbus did not. Perhaps [this
passage] should be translated as
'was happy with these signs (of
wealth) from another world'"
(Eatough, p. 240).

3   **propter vēr propinquum** Eatough
(p. 240) says "The approaching
Caribbean spring was linked to
the westerlies now blowing." Other sources give other reasons for
the timing of the departure. On
December 31 (*Diario*, p. 299) Columbus writes that he would have
preferred to continue exploring

the Hispaniola coast, "but since
he had been left with one single
ship [the *Pinta* had not yet rejoined the *Niña*] it did not seem
reasonable to expose himself to
the dangers that might happen to
him exploring." He continues on
January 3 (*Diario*, p. 305), "And
if it were certain that the caravel
Pinta would arrive safely in Spain
with that Martín Alonso Pinzón,
he would not give up doing what
he wanted to do." But not know-
ing Pinzón's whereabouts, he
feared Pinzón would reach Spain
first and tell the rulers lies to
avoid punishment for his dis-
obedience. Even on the day they
pushed off from Hispaniola for
Spain, Columbus says he passed
up a trip to other islands because
the men, worried about leaks in
the two remaining ships, wanted
to head straight home (*Diario*, p.
343, for January 16). An earlier

edition of Martyr reads *propter nostrum vēr*, "on account of *our* spring." This could mean that Columbus anticipated that if he left in mid-January, his arrival in Spain would coincide with the *Spanish* spring.

4–5 octo et trīgintā virōs . . . relīquit The leaving behind of thirty-eight men was precipitated by the loss of the *Santa María*, a connection which Martyr fails to mention. The site of the colony left behind, christened La Navidad, or of the nearby *Santa María* shipwreck, has until now not been found. But recent coordinated research by undersea explorer Barry Clifford and University of Florida archaeologist Kathleen Deagan has raised hopes that these sites are now identified. See the Discovery Channel DVD *Quest for Columbus: In Search of the Santa María* that aired in May 2004.

7–8 ictō . . . amīcitiae . . . foedere Berger (1953, p.361) defines it as "a treaty of friendship between Rome and another state establishing peaceful and friendly relations." Eatough (pp. 241–42) points out that a *foedus amīcitiae* had a special meaning in the terminology of ancient Roman Republican imperialism and suggests that this official language is meant to be linked to what happened later— when Columbus returned on his second voyage in 1493, the colony of men left behind had been wiped out. Thus the Taino could be viewed as failing to live up to a solemn obligation.

10–11 rex . . . lacrimās effūdisse vīsus est "The cacique showed much love for the Admiral and great feeling over his departure" (*Diario*, p. 301, for January 2).

13 vēla darī imperat As Columbus was laying plans to depart for Europe, the *Pinta* had not yet reappeared; hence there was a point where he was anticipating a transatlantic journey on a lone ship (*Diario*, pp. 303-05, for January 3).

14 decem virōs . . . abdūxit This statement is ambiguous, if not misleading, since Columbus had previously been engaged in abducting natives (Eatough, pp. 214 and 242; Sale, p. 122), and even admits to using force. Marx relates, "*Ego statim atque ad mare illud pervēnī, ē prīmā insulā quōsdam Indōs violenter arripuī*" (Marx, p. 11, lines 9–10). ("As soon as I came to that sea I forcibly seized some Indians from the first island.") Columbus had kidnapped natives several times. Sale estimates as many as thirty-one captives on the basis of the reports in the *Diario*. Eatough suggests that in using the number ten Martyr "may have known how many [natives] arrived in Spain."

15 nostrīs litterīs Latīnīs This effort to express native languages in the Latin alphabet implies a measure of respect accorded to those languages alongside European tongues (Eatough's note, p. 243).

AUXILIARY SENTENCES

These exercises adapted from Peter Martyr's text are designed to lead you gradually to a grasp of Martyr's prose. You may proceed either of two ways:

1) For each section, you may first read the Auxiliary Sentences and proceed to Martyr's text.

2) If you feel confident, you may read Martyr directly, and consult the Auxiliary Sentences as needed when Martyr's text presents difficulty.

- It will frequently help to consult the notes alongside Martyr's corresponding text while reading the Auxiliary Sentences.

- The Auxiliary Sentences will always be available as reference vehicles for helping explain Martyr's syntax.

- When a phrase occurs for the first time, you can often best identify and analyze it by comparing the sentence where it occurs to the previous sentence. E.g. in Section 5, compare #3 with #2, #7 with #6, #10 with #9, etc.

Auxiliary Sentences

Section 1: Columbus Obtains Royal Spanish Support and Sets Out

1. Christophorus Colōnus Fernandō suāsit sē fīnitimās Indiae insulās inventūrum esse.

2. Christophorus Colōnus Fernandō prōposuit et suāsit sē fīnitimās Indiae insulās inventūrum [esse].

3. Christophorus Colōnus Fernandō prōposuit et suāsit sē ab occidente nostrō fīnitimās Indiae insulās inventūrum.

4. Christophorus Colōnus, Ligur vir, Fernandō prōposuit et suāsit sē ab occidente nostrō fīnitimās Indiae insulās inventūrum.

5. Rex et rēgīna Colōnum nāvigiīs et aliīs rēbus instrūxērunt.

6. Rex et rēgīna Colōnum nāvigiīs et rēbus ad nāvigātiōnem pertinentibus instrūxērunt.

7. Christophorus Colōnus Fernandō prōposuit et suāsit sē fīnitimās Indiae insulās inventūrum, sī [eum] nāvigiīs et rēbus ad nāvigātiōnem pertinentibus instruerent.

8. Christiāna religiō augērī potuit.

9. Inopīnāta cōpia margarītārum arōmatumque et aurī facile potuit
    habērī.

10. Ab iīs Christiāna religiō augērī potuit, et margarītārum
    arōmatumque et aurī inopīnāta cōpia habērī facile potuit.

11. Ex rēgiō fiscō tria nāvigia destināta sunt [eī] instantī.

12. Hīs [rēbus] habitīs, ab Hispānīs lītoribus iter, institūtum cum virīs
    Hispānīs circiter CCXX, Colōnus coepit.

Section 2: The Ocean Voyage: A Restless Crew, Then Land is Sighted

1. Ab hīs igitur insulīs Colōnus nāvigāvit.

2. Ab hīs igitur insulīs Colōnus, occidentem sōlem semper secūtus,
    nāvigāvit.

3. Ab hīs igitur insulīs Colōnus, occidentem sōlem semper secūtus,
    licet in laevam paulisper, nāvigāvit.

4. Ab hīs igitur insulīs Colōnus trēs et trīginta continuōs diēs
    nāvigāvit.

5. Ab hīs igitur insulīs Colōnus trēs et trīginta continuōs diēs, coelō
    tantum et aquā contentus, nāvigāvit.

6. Mox apertīs conviciīs eum urgēbant, dē perimendō eum cōgitābant.

7. Mox apertīs convīciīs urgēbant, dē perimendō cōgitābant.

8. Mox apertīs convīciīs urgēre, dē perimendō cōgitāre.

9. Dēmum dē prōiiciendō eum in mare consulēbātur.

10. Dēmum vel dē prōiiciendō in mare consulēbātur.

11. Stimulābant hominem nē ulterius prōcēderet.

12. Ipse vērō blandīs verbīs īrātōs mulcēbat, dēpascēbat.

13. Ipse vērō blandīs modo verbīs, amplā spē modo, īrātōs mulcēbat,
    dēpascēbat.

Section 3: The Encounter with the New World Inhabitants

1. Ibi prīmum hominēs indigenās vīdērunt, quī sēsē fugientēs
    recipiunt.

2. Ibi prīmum ad terram ēgressī, hominēs indigenās vīdērunt, quī
    omnēs, factō agmine, in condensa nemora sēsē fugientēs recipiunt.

3. Ibi prīmum ad terram ēgressī, hominēs indigenās vīdērunt, quī
    venientem inaudītam gentem conspicātī, in condensa nemora sēsē
    fugientēs recipiunt.

4. Ibi prīmum ad terram ēgressī, hominēs indigenās vīdērunt, quī, factō agmine, in condensa nemora omnēs, velutī ā canibus Gallicīs timidī leporēs, sēsē fugientēs recipiunt.

5. Hanc [mulierem] cum ad nāvēs perdūxissent, nostrīs cibīs et vīnō bene saturātam, solūtam relīquērunt.

6. Hanc cum ad nāvēs perdūxissent, nostrīs cibīs et vīnō bene saturātam atque ornātam vestibus, solūtam relīquērunt.

7. Nam ea gens omnis utriusque sexūs nūda penitus vītam dūcit, nātūrā contenta.

8. Quam prīmum ad suōs mulier concessit, omnēs ad lītora certātim concurrunt.

9. Quam prīmum ad suōs mulier concessit (sciēbat enim illa quō fugientēs dīverterent), omnēs ad lītora certātim concurrunt.

10. Quam prīmum ad suōs mulier concessit, ostendissetque mīrum esse nostrōrum ornātum et līberālitātem, omnēs ad lītora certātim concurrunt.

11. Autumant gentem missam esse ē coelō.

12. Sōle ad occāsum vergente, nostrīs genua flectentibus, itidem illī faciēbant. (*There are **two** ablative absolutes here. Can you find them?*)

13. Sōle ad occāsum vergente, nostrīs, datō signō, genua flectentibus, itidem illī faciēbant. (*There are **three** ablative absolutes here. Can you find them?*)

14. Sōle ad occāsum vergente, nostrīs, datō salūtātiōnis angelicae signō, genua Christiānō rītū flectentibus, itidem illī faciēbant.

15. Quōcumque modō Christiānōs crucem colere conspicerent, eam adōrābant.

Section 4: Strange Plants and Gold Ornaments

1. Pānem ex frūmentō pānicō conficiunt.

2. Pānem ex frūmentō quōdam pānicō, cuius est apud Grānātensēs Hispānōs maxima cōpia, conficiunt.

3. Pānicula huius frūmentī longior spitamā [est], in acūtum tendens, lacertī ferē crassitūdine.

4. Grāna mīrō ordine ā nātūrā confixa sunt.

5. Torulīs auriculārum et nāribus perforātīs, aurum infertum et dīductum in tenuissimās lāminās ferunt.

6. Nostrī didicērunt mercātōrēs ad eōs nōn commeāre.

7. Nostrī didicērunt mercātōrēs ad eōs nōn commeāre, nec ipsōs alia
    lītora noscere praeter sua.

8. Cum tamen neque ad eōs commeāre mercātōrēs, nec ipsōs alia lītora
    noscere praeter sua nostrī didicissent, quaerere ab eīs coepērunt,
    unde id aurum comparārent.

9. [Indigenae dīxērunt id aurum] ex fluviōrum arēnīs lectum [esse],
    neque magnō labōre.

10. [Indigenae dīxērunt id aurum] ex fluviōrum arēnīs ab altīs montibus
    collābentibus lectum, neque magnō labōre.

Section 5: The Spanish Push Off for Home in January, 1493

1. Hīs signīs contentus, propter vēr propinquum redīre constituit.

2. Hīs igitur inventae novae tellūris signīs contentus, flantibus
    Zephyrīs, propter vēr propinquum redīre constituit.

3. Hīs igitur inventae novae tellūris signīs contentus, prosperō reditū
    flantibus Zephyrīs, propter vēr propinquum redīre constituit.

4. Hīs igitur inventae novae tellūris et inaudītī alterīus terrārum orbis
    signīs contentus, redīre constituit.

5. Octo et trīginta virōs apud eum rēgem relīquit.

6. Octo et trīginta virōs apud eum rēgem, dē quō suprā memorāvimus,
    relīquit, **ut** locōrum et temporum nātūram inquīrerent.

7. Octo et trīginta virōs apud eum rēgem, dē quō suprā memorāvimus,
    relīquit, **quī** locōrum et temporum nātūram, dōnec ipse
    reverterētur, inquīrerent.

8. Rex Guaccanarillus dē vītā et salūte ac tūtēlā eōrum, quōs ibi
    [Colōnus] relinquēbat, ēgit.

9. Rex lacrimās effūdisse vīsus est, atque omnem opem pollicitus est.

10. Misericordiā contactus ergā nostrōs, rex lacrimās effūdisse vīsus est,
    atque omnem opem pollicitus.

11. Colōnus sēcum decem virōs ex illīs abdūxit.

12. Lingua omnium illārum insulārum nostrīs litterīs Latīnīs scrībī
    poterat.

13. Lingua omnium illārum insulārum nostrīs litterīs Latīnīs sine ullō
    discrīmine scrībī poterat.

14. Colōnus sēcum decem virōs ex illīs abdūxit, ā quibus compertum
    est linguam omnium illārum insulārum nostrīs litterīs Latīnīs sine
    ullō discrīmine scrībī posse.

15. Reliqua omnia vocābula nōn minus liquidē prōferunt atque nōs,
    linguā Latīnā nostrā.

BIBLIOGRAPHY

Berger, Adolf. *Encyclopedic Dictionary of Roman Law.* Philadelphia: American Philosophical Society, 1953.

Colombo, Cristoforo. *Epistola de Insulis Nuper Inventis.* Latin text and translation by Frank E. Robbins. Ann Arbor: University Microfilms, Inc., 1966.

Columbus, Christopher. *Columbus's Letter on His First Voyage.* Edited by Walter H. Marx. N.p.: To Phrontisterion, 1972.

Columbus, Christopher. *La Carta de Colón anunciando la llegada a las Indias y a la Provincia de Catayo (China) (Descubrimiento de America): Reproducción facsimilar de las ediciones conocidas.* Intro. & Comm. by Carlos Sanz. Madrid: Gráficas Yagües, 1958.

Columbus, Christopher. *The Letter of Columbus on the Discovery of America. A Facsimile of the Pictorial Edition, with a New and Literal Translation, and a Complete Reprint of the Oldest Four Editions in Latin.* New York: Trustees of the Lenox Library, 1892.

Columbus, Christopher. *Carta de Cristóbal Colon en que da cuenta del descubrimiento de América. Edición facsimilar del texto latino publicado en Roma en 1493, con la traducción castellana.* Mexico City: Imprenta Universitaria, 1939.

Columbus, Ferdinand. *The Life of the Admiral Christopher Columbus by His Son Ferdinand.* Translated and annotated by Benjamin Keen. New Brunswick: Rutgers University Press, 1959.

Dunn, Oliver, and James E. Kelley, Jr., eds. and transs. *The* Diario *of Christopher Columbus's First Voyage to America, 1492-93: Abstracted by Fray Bartolomé de las Casas.* Norman: Univ. Of Oklahoma Press, 1989.

Fernández de Oviedo, Gonzalo. *Natural History of the West Indies.* Translated and edited by Sterling A. Stoudemire. University of North Carolina Studies in the Romance Languages and Literatures 32. Chapel Hill: Univ. of North Carolina Press, 1959.

Fernández de Oviedo, Gonzalo. *Historia general y natural de las Indias.* Edited by Juan Pérez de Tudela Bueso. 2nd ed. Biblioteca de los Autores Españoles 117. Madrid: Ediciones Atlas, 1992.

Harley, J. B. *Maps and the Columbian Encounter: An Interpretive Guide to the Travelling Exhibition*. Milwaukee: The Golda Meir Library, University of Wisconsin, 1990.

Hulme, Peter. *Colonial Encounters: Europe and the Native Caribbean, 1492–1797*. New York: Methuen, 1986.

Las Casas, Bartolomé de. *History of the Indies*. Translated and edited by Andrée Collard. N.Y.: Harper, 1971.

Las Casas, Bartolomé de. *Historia de las Indias*. Vol. 1. México: Fondo de Cultura Económica, 1951.

Morison, Samuel Eliot. *Admiral of the Ocean Sea*. Boston: Little, Brown, 1942.

Peter Martyr d'Anghera. *De Orbe Novo: The Eight decades of Peter Martyr D'Anghera*. Translated from the Latin with Notes and Introduction by Francis Augustus MacNutt. 2 vols. New York: G. Putnam's Sons, 1912.

Petrus Martyr. *De Orbe Novo Petri Martyris Anglerii ... Decades Octo*. Edited by Joachim Torres Asensio. 2 vols. Madrid: Typis Viduae et Filiae Gomez Fuentenebro, 1892.

Petrus Martyr de Angleria. *Opera. Legatio Babylonica. De Orbe Novo Decades Octo. Opus Epistolarum*. Graz: Akademische Druck- u. Verlagsanstalt, 1966. (Contains facsimile of *editio Complutense* of *De Orbe Novo*, 1530.)

Rouse, Irving. *The Tainos: Rise & Decline of the People Who Greeted Columbus*. New Haven: Yale Univ. Press, 1992.

Sale, Kirkpatrick. *The Conquest of Paradise*. New York: Alfred A. Knopf, 1990.

Sauer, Carl O. *The Early Spanish Main*. Berkeley: Univ. of California Press, 1966.

Symcox, Geoffrey, et al., ed. *Repertorium Columbianum*. Vol. 5, *Selections from Peter Martyr*, edited and translated by Geoffrey Eatough. Published under the Auspices of the UCLA Center for Medieval and Renaissance Studies. Turnhout, Belgium: Brepols, 1998.

Torres, Alberto J. *Peso y medidas antiguas en México*. Historia: Documentos e Investigación, no. 31. Guadalajara: Gobierno del Estado de Jalisco, 1987.

LATIN TO ENGLISH LEXICON

A

acerbus, -a, -um, bitter; *here* "immature, still growing" (Section 4, line 6)

adorior, adorīrī, adortus sum, to assault, to attack

adōrō, adōrāre, adōrāvī, adōrātum, to adore

aemulor, aemulārī, aemulātus sum, to imitate; to be like

aestimātiō, aestimatiōnis, f. value

agmen, agminis, n. a moving throng; a mass of people on the move

albeō, albēre, to be white

aliquī, aliqua, aliquod, some

arēna, -ae, f. sand

arōma, arōmatis, n. spice

attineō, attinēre, attinuī, attentum, to pertain, to be pertinent

augeō, augēre, auxī, auctum, to spread, to increase

aureus, -a, -um, golden

auricula, -ae, f. ear

autumō, autumāre, autumāvī, autumātum, to affirm

B

blandus, -a, -um, soft, soothing

C

caelum, -ī, n. sky (sometimes written *coelum, -ī,* n.)

candor, candōris, m. whiteness

caravella, -ae, f. sailing ship, caravel

certātim, (adv.) in competition (with each other)

circiter, (adv.) nearly, approximately

collābor, collābī, collapsus sum, to come tumbling down

colō, colere, coluī, cultus, to venerate, to pay honor to, to worship

comes, comitis, m./f. companion, fellow traveler

commeō, commeāre, commeāvī, commeātum, to come and go, to travel

comparō, comparāre, comparāvī, comparātum, to procure

comperiō, comperīre, comperī, compertum, to learn

complector, complectī, complexus sum, to embrace

concēdō, concēdere, concessī, concessum, to go away

condensus, -a, -um, dense

configō, configere, confīxī, confixum, to fasten, to join together

conspicor, conspicārī, conspicātus sum, to catch sight of

contineō, continēre, continuī, contentum, to surround.

contentus, -a, -um, content (+ abl.); surrounded (+abl.)

contingō, contingere, contigī, contactum, to touch

convīcium, -iī, n. insult, abuse

crassitūdō, crassitūdinis, f. thickness

crux, crucis, f. the Christian cross

D

dēmum, (adv.) finally

dēpascō, dēpascere, dēpāvī, dēpastum, to feed (e.g. one's hopes)

dēserō, dēserere, deseruī, dēsertum, to desert

destinō, destināre, destināvī, destinātum, to appoint, to designate, to allocate

dīdūcō, dīdūcere, dīdūxī, dīductum, to draw out, to spread

dīrigō, dīrigere, dīrēxī, dīrectum, to direct

discō, discere, didicī, to learn, to find out

discrīmen, discrīminis, n. difference; danger, risk, hazard, discrepancy; difficulty

dīvertō, dīvertere, dīvertī, dīversum, to separate oneself, to depart

dōnec, (conj. foll. by subjv.) until

E

ecce, (adv.) behold! look!

efficiō, efficere, effēcī, effectum, to make, to form; to complete

effundō, effundere, effūdī, effūsum, to pour out, to shed

ēgredior, ēgredī, ēgressus sum, to disembark, to land

ergā, (+ acc.) toward

exsuperō, exsuperāre, exsuperāvī, exsuperātum, to surpass

F

ferē, (adv.) approximately

ferō, ferre, tulī, lātum, here "to wear" (Section 4, line 11)

fiscus, -ī, m. treasury

flectō, flectere, flexī, flexum, to bend

flō, flāre, flāvī, flātum, to blow

G

Gallicus, -a, -um, Gallic; *Canis Gallicus* = a breed of hunting dog

genū, genūs, n. knee

Grānātensēs Hispānī, Grānātensium Hispānōrum, m.pl. inhabitants of the region of Andalusia in Spain; people of Granada

grānum, -ī, n. kernel, grain

Guaccanarillus, - ī, m. Guacanagarí, the chieftain met by Columbus

H

Hispānus, -a, -um, Spanish

honōrificē, (adv.) with honor

I

iciō, icere, īcī, ictum, to strike; *foedus icere* = to conclude a treaty

incola, -ae, m./f. inhabitant

indigena, -ae, m./f. inhabitant; native

inferciō, infercīre, infersī, infertum, to insert; to stuff

inopīnātus, -a, -um, unexpected, unanticipated

insequor, insequī, insecūtus sum, to follow

instituō, instituere, instituī, institūtum, to put together, to organize

instō, instāre, institī, instātum, to press, to insist, to demand

instruō, instruere, instrūxī, instructum, to equip, to outfit (+ acc. and abl.); to instruct (i.e. in the truths of Christianity)

Insubrēs, -ium, m. pl. Insubrians = people from the region of Milan in Italy

invenio, invenīre, invēnī, inventum, to find

Ioanna, -ae, f. Cuba; in Spanish, *Juana*

iter, itineris, n. path

itidem, (adv.) likewise

K

Kal. = Kalendae, -ārum, f. pl. the Ca-
lends, the first day of the month

L

lacertus, -ī, m. upper arm

laetus, -a, -um, rejoicing, happy, glad

laevus, -a, -um, the left (i.e. south, to a
voyager traveling west)

lāmina, -ae, f. sheet

legō, legere, lēgī, lectum, to collect,
to gather

lepus, leporis, m. hare

līberālitās, līberālitātis, f. generos-
ity, gift

licet, (conj.) although

Ligur, Liguris, of Liguria, the region
around Genoa in Italy

liquidē, (adv.) clearly

litterae, -ārum, f. pl., *here,* alphabet
letters (Section 5, line 15)

lītus, lītoris, n. shore

M

maizium, -ī, n. maize

margarīta, -ae, f. pearl

mātūrescō, mātūrescere, mātūruī,
to mature, to become ripe

mercātōrius, -a, -um, for merchant
trade

millēsimus, -a, -um, one thousandth

mīrus, -a, -um, wonderful; remarkable; amazing

misereor, misererī, miseritus sum
to have pity on (+ dat.)

misericordia, -ae, f. compassion,
pity

modo . . . modo . . ., first . . . then . . .

modus, -ī, m. way, manner

mulceō, mulcēre, mulsī, mulsum, to
soothe, to stroke

murmurō, murmurāre, murmurāvī,
murmurātum, to grumble

N

nāris, nāris, f. nostril; pl., nose

nāvigātiō, nāvigātiōnis, f. sailing

nāvigium, -ī, n. vessel

nemus, nemoris, n. grove, woods

niger, nigra, nigrum, black, dark

nix, nivis, f. snow

nōbilis, -e, renowned (+ abl. of the
cause of renown)

nōnāgēsimus, -a, -um, ninetieth

O

occāsus, occāsūs, m. setting (of the
sun)

occidens, occidentis, m. the west

occidō, occidere, occidī, occāsum,
to set, to sink down

onerārius, -a, -um, of burden, of
transport, for cargo

optō, optāre, optāvī, optātum, to ex-
pect, to wait for

ornātus, ornātūs, m. attire, garb

P

pānicula, -ae, f. head; ear (of grain)

pānicum, -ī, n. Italian millet, *setaria
italica,* or "panic-grass;" (see background note to Section 5, line 1)

patefaciō, patefacere, patefēcī, patefactum, to expose, to bring to light

paulisper, (adv.) for a little while, for
a short time

penitus, (adv.) completely, entirely

percieō, percière, percīvī, percītum,
to stir up, to excite

perforō, perforāre, perforāvī, perforātum, to perforate

perimō, perimere, perēmī, peremptum, to kill

pīsum legūmen, pīsī legūminis, n. pea

polliceor, pollicērī, pollicitus sum, to promise

praeter, (+ acc.) beyond, in addition to

prōclāmō, prōclāmāre, prōclāmāvī, prōclāmātum, to insist, to cry out

prōferō, prōferre, prōtulī, prōlātum, to pronounce, to utter, to express

prōiciō, prōicere, proiēcī, proiectum, to throw out, to throw overboard

prōpōnō, prōpōnere, prōposuī, prōpositum, to propose

prospectus, prospectūs, m. sight

prosperus, -a, -um, favorable, successful, prosperous

prōtrahō, prōtrahere, prōtrāxī, prōtractum, to drag out, to extend

Q

quadringentēsimus, -a, -um, four hundredth

quīcumque, quaecumque, quodcumque, whoever, whatever

quīdam, quaedam, quoddam, a certain, a kind of

quō, (adv.) whither, to where

R

recipiō, recipere, recēpī, receptum, to receive; with se, to escape to, to retreat to, to take refuge in (+ in, ad + acc.)

reditus, reditūs, m. return, going back

rēgius, -a, -um, royal

revertor, revertī, reversus sum, to return, to go back

rītus, rītūs, m. rite

S

saturō, saturāre, saturāvī, saturātum, to fill

September, Septembris, of September

sequor, sequī, secūtus sum, to follow

solvō, solvere, solvī, solūtum, to release, to liberate

spitama, -ae, f. a measure of length, a span (c. 224 mm.); sometimes spelled *spithama*

stimulō, stimulāre, stimulāvī, stimulātum, to urge

suādeō, suādēre, suāsī, to persuade (+ dat.)

suī, sibī, sē, sē, himself, herself, itself, themselves

suscipiō, suscipere, suscēpī, susceptum, to welcome, to receive, to absorb

T

tacitus, -a, -um, silent

tantum, (adv.) only, just

tellūs, tellūris, f. land

tendō, tendere, tetendī, tentum, to reach, to expand, to stretch

timidus, -a, -um, timid, fearful

torulus, -ī, m. *here*, "lobe" (Section 4, line 10)

trīcēsimus, -a, -um, thirtieth

tūtēla, -ae, f. protection

U

ulterius, (adv.) any further

ūnā, (adv.) at the same time, together

unde, (adv.) from where

urgeō, urgēre, ursī, to encourage

V

-ve, (enclitic) and

vel, (adv.) or; even

vēlum, -ī, n. sail; *vēla dare* = "to set sail"

velutī, (adv.) just as, like

vendicō, vendicāre, vendicāvī, vendicātum, to revenge oneself; (in classical Latin, spelled *vindicō*)

veneror, venerārī, venerātus sum, to venerate

ventus, - ī , m. wind

vēr, vēris, n. spring

vergō, vergere, to incline, to turn; *here,* to sink (Section 3, line 15)

vocābulum, -ī, n. word

vocō, vocāre, vocāvī, vocātum, to call, to call in the sense of "to name" (Section 5, line 16).

Z

Zephyrus, -ī, m. west wind

BRIDGES TO READING COMPREHENSION

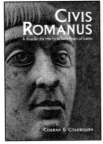

CIVIS ROMANUS
A Reader for the First Two Years of Latin
by Cobban and Colebourn

Civis Romanus is a graded Latin reader for beginning Latin students. The memorable stories that grew from the civilization of ancient Rome are the basis of the Latin passages in this unique reader. Thus students read about actual people and events while honing their Latin grammatical and syntactical skills and increasing their Latin vocabulary. Students who finish this reader in beginning Latin (Latin 1 and 2 at the high school level) will have acquired a minimum vocabulary of 1,000 words.

xii + 128 pp.
(2003 reprint of 1967 edition)
6" x 9" Paperback,
ISBN 978-0-86516-569-4

FEATURES OF THE TEXT:

- new introduction by Marianthe Colakis

- 60 passages of graded Latin readings of graduated length (from 120 to 300 words) on Roman legends, people in Roman government, Roman daily life, historical figures, and famous events

- special Latin-to-English vocabulary list for each reading
- general Latin-to-English glossary
- list of grammar assumed for each reading
- Key that contains the literal translations of each reading is available

---

VERGIL
A Legamus Transitional Reader
by Thomas J. Sienkewicz and LeaAnn A. Osburn

This reader contains selections (about 200 lines) from Vergil's *Aeneid*, Books I, II, and IV, and is designed for students moving from elementary or intermediate Latin into reading the authentic Latin of Vergil.

FEATURES OF THE TEXT:

- pre-reading materials for each passage of Latin, designed to help the student understand the underlying cultural and literary concepts in the Latin passage.

- short explanations related to the grammatical and syntactical usages that will be found in the passage, accompanied by exercises.

xxiv + 136 pp.
(2004) 8 ½" x 11" Paperback,
ISBN 978-0-86516-578-6

- first version of the Latin text with gapped words in parentheses and difficult noun-adjective pairings highlighted by the use of a different font
- complete vocabulary and grammatical notes on the page facing the Latin passage. Any vocabulary word found in the passage but not in the notes is found in the pull-out vocabulary at the back of the book
- second version of the Latin text in its unchanged form with literary notes on the facing page
- post-reading materials for each passage designed to help the student understand Vergil's style of writing and to allow the student to reflect upon what has been read
- last four Latin passages without any of the transitional aids such as gapped words or the use of fonts. Notes on grammar, vocabulary, and literary analysis continue to be on the page facing the passage

BOLCHAZY-CARDUCCI PUBLISHERS, INC.
WWW.BOLCHAZY.COM